HISTORY IN DEPTH

WOMEN IN WORLD WAR I

Stuart Sillars

M
MACMILLAN
EDUCATION

For Duncan and Hazel

First published 1987

Published by
MACMILLAN EDUCATION LTD
Houndmills, Basingstoke, Hampshire RG21 2XS
and London
Companies and representatives
throughout the world

Printed in Hong Kong

British Library Cataloguing in Publication Data
Sillars, Stuart
Women in World War I—(History in depth)
1. World War, 1914–1918—Women
I. Title   II. Series
940.3′15′042   D639.W7
ISBN 0–333–42315–1

CONTENTS

Preface   4

1 The right to serve   5

2 Women at work   17

3 Change at home and work   37

4 Women and politics   47

   Index   56

Acknowledgements

The author would like to thank Peter H. Liddle for his kindness and generosity in making available his Personal Experience Archives; Dr C.W.M. Pratt, Pembroke College, Cambridge; Dr David Stephenson, Academic Director, Cambridge Seminars; Mrs Jan Hillier; and the staff of Cambridge University Library for their help in the preparation of this book.

The author and publishers wish to acknowledge, with thanks, the following photographic sources:

BBC Hulton Picture Library frontispiece and pp 8, 10, 18, 22, 24, 28, 30, 31, 44, 45, 47, 52 top and bottom, 53 top and bottom, 54–5 top; Cambridge University Library pp 12 left, 19; *Illustrated London News* p 39; Imperial War Museum pp 9, 26; Peter Liddle p 37; Mansell Collection pp 5, 12 right, 16, 48; John Topham Picture Library pp 34, 40, 42 top and bottom, 43, 49, 54–5 bottom; *The War Illustrated* pp 13, 21, 27, 35.

The publishers have made every effort to trace the copyright holders, but if they have inadvertently overlooked any, they will be pleased to make the necessary arrangements at the first opportunity.

PREFACE

The study of history is exciting, whether in a good story well told, a mystery solved by the judicious unravelling of clues, or a study of the men, women and children whose fears and ambitions, successes and tragedies make up the collective memory of mankind.

This series aims to reveal this excitement to pupils through a set of topic books on important historical subjects from the Middle Ages to the present day. Each book contains four main elements: a narrative and descriptive text, lively and relevant illustrations, extracts of contemporary evidence, and questions for further thought and work. Involvement in these elements should provide an adventure which will bring the past to life in the imagination of the pupil.

Each book is also designed to develop the knowledge, skills and concepts so essential to a pupil's growth. It provides a wide, varying introduction to the evidence available on each topic. In handling this evidence, pupils will increase their understanding of basic historical concepts such as causation and change, as well as of more advanced ideas such as revolution and democracy. In addition, their use of basic study skills will be complemented by more sophisticated historical skills such as the detection of bias and the formulation of opinion.

The intended audience for the series is pupils of eleven to sixteen years: it is expected that the earlier topics will be introduced in the first three years of secondary school, while the nineteenth and twentieth century topics are directed towards first examinations.

THE RIGHT TO SERVE

1

Saturday 17 July 1915: Victoria Embankment, London. There is heavy rain. Gradually a crowd of women assembles, growing until it stretches the length of the embankment. Three hundred marshals wearing red sashes organise the crowd into 125 sections. There are 700 women carrying banners and 90 brass bands: the crowd numbers many thousands. At 3.30 p.m. a bugle rings out. The bands strike up, and the procession moves off, headed by a woman carrying the flags of the Allied nations. She is followed by another woman who, barefoot in the rain and dirt of the road, represents Belgium, invaded by Germany but undefeated in spirit.

The 'Women's Right-to-Serve Procession', organised by Christabel Pankhurst and the Women's Social and Political Union, is the largest demonstration of women seen in London since the suffragette meetings before the war. The procession turns at the Houses of Parliament and passes down Whitehall, where it is watched by Lloyd George, Minister of Munitions, and Winston Churchill, First Lord of the Admiralty. It moves on through London, watched by people glad of something colourful after long dreary months of war. At

The 'Right-to-Serve' procession

6 p.m. the procession returns to the embankment; it is now estimated to be 60 000 strong. The women crowd into the gardens of the Ministry of Munitions and hear speeches from Christabel Pankhurst and Lloyd George. The Minister of Munitions assures them that they will play their part in winning the war: 'Without women, victory will tarry, and a victory that tarries means a victory whose footprints are footprints of blood.' There is cheering: hats, handkerchiefs and flags are waved. Then slowly the women disperse, assured that their aim has been achieved, leaving London to its blacked-out, wartime night.

Work, work, work!

The procession was one of the most obvious signs of a growing desire among women to become more involved in the war effort. Christabel Pankhurst, announcing the meeting, said that it would:

> ... have the effect of showing the Government that women are ready; it will also have the effect, the moral effect, of showing the men of the country that the women are not one whit behind them in patriotism.
>
> The Suffragette, 9 July 1915

After the procession, Lloyd George told Christabel Pankhurst that he would give women every opportunity to contribute to the war, and assured her that they would not be used as a source of cheap labour – so the procession would seem to have succeeded. Also, if press reports are to be believed, the march had convinced the nation of the women's determination, and their right to help in the war effort. Here are two accounts:

> To call it historic – this procession of wives and mothers, matrons and girls, all demanding the right to serve – is not enough. It is the first time in history that the womanhood of England, or, indeed, of any country, has made so simple, so spontaneous, so overwhelming a manifestation of its dauntless and undivided spirit.
>
> The Daily Chronicle, 19 July 1915

> They were women of all classes – ladies of title, working women, and, in the majority, women and girls of the middle classes – all eager, as the battle-cry of one of their hundred banners had it, to 'work, work, work'.
>
> The Observer, 18 July 1915

Questions

1 What does Christabel Pankhurst's statement reveal about her opinion of women's attitudes towards the war and the men who were fighting it?

2 Why do you think the press reports stress that women of all kinds joined the procession? Look at the illustration on page 5, then say whether you think the claim was true.

3 Look again at the press reports of the procession. How would you describe the writers' attitudes towards women? Support your answer by quoting appropriate words and phrases.

Successful though the procession seemed, not everyone agreed with it. Sylvia Pankhurst, for example, formed her own rival procession. Unlike her mother and sister, she did not support the war. She was angry that reports of the march had implied that it represented the opinions of all women. She was also furious that the march had been paid for largely by a Government grant. The banners carried on her march expressed anger that women were being paid poor wages while employers made large profits. The slogans included: 'No National Service under makers of Private Profit!'; 'A Man's Wage for a Man's Job!'; and 'Down with High Prices and Big Profits!'

Questions

1 How is your view of the 'Right-to-Serve' procession affected by the fact that the Government largely paid for it?

2 Look again at the slogans displayed on Sylvia Pankhurst's march. What kind of people do you think they would have appealed to?

3 What do these two marches warn the historian against doing when considering the roles and attitudes of women during World War I?

It is clear from Sylvia Pankhurst's reactions that the 'Right-to-Serve' procession was not a spontaneous, united display of the feelings of the women of the nation. It was only one part of a larger movement of protest about the exclusion of women from war work. To understand this movement, we must look at how women of all kinds reacted to the coming of war, and the part which they played in it during the early months of fighting.

'... go home and sit still'

Women had been campaigning since the end of the nineteenth century for a greater involvement in the public life of the nation. The most dramatic form of protest was seen in the campaigns for votes for women led by the Women's Social and Political Union (WSPU). This was headed by Mrs Emmeline Pankhurst, the mother of

Christabel and Sylvia. The more militant members of the WSPU had chained themselves to railings, set fire to pillar boxes, hurled bricks through windows and attacked MPs and policemen at demonstrations. When imprisoned, they had gone on hunger strike and endured the barbaric horrors of forcible feeding. All this showed the depth and intensity of their desire to obtain the vote, and so gain a voice in the nation's affairs.

Another important organisation was the National Union of Women's Suffrage Societies (NUWSS). It had been formed in 1897 – six years before the formation of the WSPU – to bring together the activities of many separate groups throughout the country which were campaigning for votes for women. It had a much larger membership than the WSPU, and its methods were different. Instead of violent action, it favoured peaceful persuasion, and was careful to call its members 'suffragists' to distinguish them from the militant 'suffragettes'. Many of its members were pacifists who became involved in action to try to stop the war or to help those who refused to fight – a strong contrast to the WSPU's wholehearted and passionate support of the fighting. Despite their different methods, however, the two organisations had the same aim: to increase the part played by women in national life.

This aim must be seen against a wider background of change in the opportunities open to women during the early years of the twentieth century. Women had begun to be admitted to some universities; the first women doctors had gone into practice; and women secretaries had begun to take over the work traditionally done by

From campaigning for the vote to campaigning for the war. Below left: a meeting in favour of votes for women, 1908. Below right: a recruitment meeting, 1915

male clerks. Taken together, these movements show the growing desire among women of all backgrounds to become actively involved in all areas of civil and commercial life.

By the outbreak of war in 1914 this desire had reached a high point. It found expression in many forms. For many women of the upper and middle classes, the wish for a more active life was combined with intense patriotism. Society ladies rode through Hyde Park with army recruitment posters tied to their saddles; famous singers and actresses addressed meetings in city centres, urging young men to enlist. Some women became involved in fund raising, or in collecting and sending parcels of 'comforts' – books, chocolates, cigarettes, socks and similar items – to soldiers at the front, while others sewed shirts or sandbags.

Many women, particularly those whose husbands had small businesses, became involved in more practical ways. As the men went off to fight, the women took over their jobs; they became plumbers, window-cleaners and chimney sweeps, and did many other types of work previously only done by men. Enthusiastic reports appeared in the press about the involvement of women in this way. Women of the Red Cross, who had long ago established the right to follow their chosen profession, responded very rapidly. The first detachment of nurses arrived in France only weeks after war had been declared, to the accompaniment of press headlines about 'Angels of Mercy'. Nursing was one area in which there was no male opposition to women's involvement, but in other areas women met with far less encouragement.

An early recruitment poster. What do you think is the relationship between the woman and the man? What kind of pressure is being put on men to join up? Do you think it is fair?

Sewing shirts for sailors

Many highly qualified women who wished to help the war effort were denied the chance to do so. In 1918 Lady Frances Balfour recalled the first year of the war:

> *The Suffrage organisations, staffed and equipped with able practical women Jacks of all trades, in their midst, put themselves at the call of national service, but were headed back from all enterprises. It had been ordained that women could not fight, and therefore they were of no use in war time.*
>
> Lady Frances Balfour: *Dr Elsie Inglis*, 1918

The same writer goes on to describe the experience of Dr Elsie Inglis, who offered her medical skills for the war effort to a departmental head at the War Office:

> *Official reserve at last gave way, and the historic sentence was uttered – 'My good lady, go home and sit still.'*

It was not only highly trained women who were denied the opportunity to serve. Ironically, many working-class women had known greater freedom than their middle-class sisters before the war, since they had jobs of their own – though their reason for working was sheer financial need rather than the desire for an independent career. When war came, many of the two million women working in factories were thrown out of work when the demand for textiles – the largest area of employment – was reduced. Some switched from making clothes to making munitions; yet this change took place without any control or intervention from the Government, who were reluctant to become involved in organising or harnessing women's efforts in the early stages of the war.

Why was Asquith's Government reluctant to allow women to become involved in war work? One important reason was that it doubted their ability to perform many physically or intellectually demanding jobs. It also mistrusted the women's emancipation movement, associating it mainly with the 'suffragette outrages'. Perhaps, too, it feared action from the trade unions; the years before the war had seen many serious strikes, and the widespread employment of women might well cause further disruption by men who felt their jobs were at risk. But possibly the main reason was that it did not fully understand the enormity of the war and its effect on the nation.

These reasons, and the attitudes behind them, were to have important repercussions as the war drew into its second year. At the start of the war, however, it was clear that although women of all classes and backgrounds wanted to be involved in the nation's war effort, the Government did little to make this possible, and in many cases deliberately rejected their offers of help.

Questions

1   List the jobs which women did during the first months of the war.

2   What differences have you noticed in the roles played by women from different social classes in the first months of the war?

The pressure for war work

As the first New Year of the war began, a mood of increasing impatience began to be felt among women of all backgrounds. Women who had given up their battle to win the vote in order to help win the war had been offered only comparatively unimportant jobs as gardeners or drivers; and those with high qualifications and special skills had not been allowed to use them. It seemed that, with very few exceptions, women would be allowed to play only a minor part in the war effort.

The Government tried to satisfy the growing demand for work with a scheme under which women could register for war work. The official announcement of the scheme said this about it:

The object of registration is to find out what reserve of women's labour, trained or untrained, can be made available if required. As ... openings for employment present themselves, notice will be given through the Labour Exchanges, with full details as to the nature of work, conditions, and pay, and, so far as special training is necessary, arrangements will, if possible, be made for the purpose.

Any woman who by working helps to release a man or to equip a man for fighting does national war service. Every woman should register who is able and willing to take employment.

Official statement published in *The Times*, 18 March 1915

"WE SHOULD MISS YOU, MARY, BUT YOUR UNDOUBTED TALENT SHOULD BE OFFERED TO THE NATION IF THERE IS A WOMAN'S BOMB-DROPPING CORPS."

Above: *women registering for war work*

Right: *a cartoon from* Punch *– a magazine for upper- and middle-class men – 18 August 1915*

Questions

1 What impression does this announcement give of how important the Government felt the employment of women was? Quote words and phrases to support your answer.

2 Do you think this attitude is also shown in the arrangement of the recruiting stall shown in the illustration on this page? Give reasons for your answer.

The voluntary registration scheme did little to satisfy the demands of the women, or to calm their anger, because it gave no definite commitment to employ women in greater numbers. In April, a Conference of Women's Organisations was held at the Board of Trade, with the aim of gaining their help in Government programmes of recruitment and training. Many of the groups disagreed with each other's aims, but they still agreed to help. From this it is clear that women from a wide range of backgrounds wanted to take a more active part in the war, and were angry at the Government's lack of interest. They wanted to help for patriotic reasons, but they also had other motives, as one historian points out:

... owing to the increased cost of living and the breaking up of homes, women who had never previously earned their living desired to work partly because they considered it right to do so, and so to free

men for active service, and partly because ... it became necessary for them to earn something.

Mrs C.S. Peel: *How We Lived Then, 1914–1918,* 1929

Questions

1 What are the two main reasons given here for women's desire for war work?

2 Do you think they were equally important for all women who wanted war work?

3 Can you think of any reasons why the Government was reluctant to allow women to become more involved in war work?

Women in munitions

While thousands of women clamoured for work, those few who did have jobs often worked dangerously long hours.

At Greenwood and Batley's armament factory in Leeds, a girl, only sixteen years of age, was injured at her machine. She had started at

A munitions factory in Leeds in 1915 – possibly Greenwood and Batley's. How does the contemporary caption compare with the ideas expressed by the magistrate in the Pankhurst passage on page 14?

PATRIOTIC women and girl workers are labouring hard every day, and often all night, in order to provide cartridges for our soldiers at the front.

6 a.m. Friday, and with intervals totalling two hours for meals on Friday, and half an hour for breakfast on Saturday, she had kept on till the accident occurred at 7.30 a.m. The women beside her worked on for 31 hours. On being prosecuted, the manager stated, by way of defence, that women subjected to this tremendous strain would earn from £1 to £2 a week. The magistrate, Horace Marshall, dismissed the case, with the observation that 'the most important thing in the world today is that ammunition shall be made'. The senseless folly of this overwork was revealed when, on 21st May, it was announced that 65,700 women had registered for war service, but only 1,250 of them had received employment.

Sylvia Pankhurst: *The Home Front*, 1932

Questions

1 In what way did the firm feel that the need for munitions allowed them to change their employees' working conditions? Did the magistrate approve of what the firm was doing?

2 What do the registration and employment figures suggest about:
   a) women's response to the voluntary register
   b) the Government's attitude to employing women?

What the historian must ask here is why more women were not employed in making munitions at a time when the country was desperately in need of them. There were two main reasons. First, employers wanted to produce as much as possible for the lowest cost in wages, even when it meant that women had to work for far longer than the ten hours a day which had been set as a maximum by the Factory Act of 1874. As we have seen, they used the excuse that such efforts were necessary in war, when it was important to produce munitions quickly and cheaply.

Secondly, trade unions saw the employment of women as a threat to men's jobs. After a long struggle they had achieved fixed pay and tolerable conditions of work in many industries, and they were unwilling now to lose their jobs to unskilled women who, they feared, would be paid less and would therefore be kept on after the war.

Some employers made agreements with the unions. These stressed that 'dilution' – the employment of 'unskilled' men or women to do skilled jobs – would only occur during the war. After the fighting, skilled men would get their jobs back on pre-war terms. In March 1915 the Treasury Agreement was signed. It extended the private agreements to cover all munitions factories.

The Treasury Agreement was an advance in some ways, but many women were angry that they had not been consulted before it was signed. Others feared that women would be paid by the hour, instead of earning the 'piece rates' – a separate sum for each item produced – which men received. Sylvia Pankhurst, a lifelong campaigner for equal pay, summed up the general feeling:

> *It was a fact that not merely the Government and other employers, but also the leaders of Trade Unionism for women, regarded equal pay as an impossible demand. To many it seemed an outrageously extravagant demand, above all during the war, that single women should be paid the wage that a man with a family might exact. Our hard, vain efforts for equal pay brought home to me, as so often before, the supreme difficulty of securing under the wage system a decent subsistence for the woman who is the bread-winner of a family. In the great average she is crushed down to the wage level on which the single woman finds it just possible to subsist.*
>
> Sylvia Pankhurst: *The Home Front*, 1932

subsistence: living wage

Questions

1 What does 'dilution' of workers mean? What attitude towards unskilled workers, both male and female, does this word suggest to you?

2 Look again at the extract from Sylvia Pankhurst's book. Why did many people feel that men and women should not have equal pay? Do you think that the circumstances under which women were employed during the war were any justification for paying them less than men?

In the end it was not the Treasury Agreement but a completely different series of events which led directly to the employment of more women. Many people were dissatisfied with the way Asquith's Liberal Government was handling the war, and *The Times* and the *Daily Mail* ran campaigns accusing it of not producing enough shells. Asquith was forced to form a coalition, and to create a Ministry of Munitions with Lloyd George at its head.

Now, at last, events began to move quickly. The Ministry took over all existing arms factories, built new ones, and introduced controls on employment. Above all, it began to employ more women.

It was at this point that the 'Right-to-Serve' procession took place – when most of the advances had already been won. In the next 12 months, 264 000 women were recruited to munitions work. Where munitions led, others followed. There were still disagreements about pay and conditions, but now it seemed that women were at last being allowed to take on the larger role they had desired since the war began. As they did so, they showed that they could perform all kinds of work once thought to be the preserve of men. In consequence, attitudes to women began to change:

Hostess. "THIS IS MY YOUNGEST DAUGHTER. SHE MAKES MUNITIONS ALL DAY."
Visitor. "HOW NICE! ALL GIRLS SHOULD BE DOING SOMETHING FOR THE WAR. I DISAPPROVE OF SLACKERS. MY DEAR GIRL
NEARLY *KILLS* HERSELF SELLING FLAGS."

A cartoon from Punch,
5 July 1916

Before the year was out the new use of female labour was being
extended to industries other than those directly involved in the manu-
facture of munitions, and the Board of Trade had increased its
strength of women factory inspectors by 50 per cent. These develop-
ments in the main were limited to working-class women, although
when the Ministry of Munitions' recruitment of 'munitions girls' got
under way many of the delicate products of middle- and upper-class
homes were found to possess a remarkable toughness and resilience.

Arthur Marwick: *The Deluge*, 1965

Questions

1   What kind of people is the author referring to in the phrase
'delicate products of middle- and upper-class homes'? What do
you think is his attitude towards them?

2   Draw up a table like the one started below, listing all the
sources quoted in this chapter. Put a tick in the column or
columns which describe the kind of material each extract
contains: fact, opinion or attitude.

Source	Fact	Opinion	Attitude
The Suffragette	—	√	√

3   Compare the two *Punch* cartoons. What does the difference
between them suggest about the way attitudes to women in
war work had changed between August 1915 and July 1916?

2 | WOMEN AT WORK

Munitions

I stood in a glass-sided passage and looked out over a vast shop blazing with light, humming with belts and machinery, packed with lathes and their women workers, brilliant with the vivid colouring of the flags – Union Jacks and Standards – that were hoisted proudly over the head of each girl and her machine. The girls were in khaki overalls and caps, and the massed colours of the khaki, of the Allied flags' scarlet and blue and white and orange and black, the glistening steely-blue of the machinery, the warm touches of the red copper and yellow brass, all under the bright glow of the electrics, all jostling and astir and quivering with life and animated movement, made up a picture as thrilling and alive and heart-warming as any I have seen throughout the war works ... There are 7,000 girls at work there now; they average 87½ hours' work a week, and they are 'as steady as rocks, as regular and reliable as the factory hooter'.

'Boyd Cable': *Doing Their Bit*, 1916

Questions

1 Compare this passage with the illustration on the cover of this book – *For King and Country* by E.F. Skinner, an official war artist. What similarities and what differences can you find?

2 Both the writer and the artist were employed by Government departments to record the work of women. Do you think this influenced the way they presented what they saw?

3 Compare the passage above and the cover painting with the illustration on page 18. What differences are there?

The extract from *Doing Their Bit* is typical of many books and articles in its glowing praise of women munition workers, but there was another side to the work it describes – one of hardship and sacrifice.

By the end of the war, one woman in 20 was working in munitions. Some worked in their home towns, but many had to leave family and friends and go to new areas, such as the specially built town of huts at Gretna in Scotland, which housed 9 000 women and 3 000 men. They travelled to work in special trains, herded into 'Ladies Only' carriages by policewomen, or on foot, leaving early in the morning to be at work on time. Often they carried small cardboard cases holding their overalls, and perhaps some sandwiches to save 5d. (2½p) – the price of a plate of mince and vegetables in the canteen. In some areas the 'Khaki Girls' were searched by police-women when they arrived at work, since hairpins or matches could cause explosions.

Shifts usually lasted for 12 hours, starting at seven in the morning and seven at night. Weekly pay rose from 15 shillings (75p) in 1914 to 35 shillings (£1.75) in 1918, and overtime or night-shift work might well double this figure. A woman who was 20 minutes late would lose a 'quarter' – 2½ hours' pay. Anyone who stopped work before the hooter sounded would be fined 2s.6d. (12½p). Although the press often carried stories of 'munitionettes' wearing fur coats and buying expensive luxuries with their excessive earnings, most women had little money left after paying for their lodgings, food and travel.

Day after day in the factories many women worked at turning or grinding shell-cases, standing at their machines on wooden platforms which raised them above the 'swarf' – razor-sharp spirals of waste metal cut from the shells. Women supervisors inspected the work, and in some factories men set up and adjusted the machines. Occasionally, a man who was too old to fight in the war would sluice floors with water and disinfectant. In the older factories, this would stand in hollows in the concrete, mingling with swarf, discarded rags and 'mystic', the fluid used to cool hot machinery. When Zeppelins (airships) or bombers were directly overhead, the women would take shelter, but otherwise they stayed at their work throughout the air raids.

Work with explosives was especially dangerous, even though workers wore respirators, veils and other protective clothing. Pro-

Turning a shell-case, 1915. What safety hazards can you see here, and what precautions are being taken against them?

longed exposure to TNT, an important ingredient in explosives, caused toxic jaundice, an illness which turned the skin yellow, earning those who worked with the substance the nickname of 'canaries'. The consequences of this could be very serious:

Not only did Jenny become yellow; she found after a time that the powder was affecting her skin. Her face, neck and legs began to swell, so much so that she could not see and had to be led home. She was ordered to stay home for ten days on half pay. For three days she could not see anything. On being examined by the works doctor, TNT poisoning was diagnosed. This was something Jenny had not bargained for. She had to be bandaged, as the skin had now broken and the fluid was escaping; she looked like a member of the Ku Klux Klan or an Egyptian mummy for some time. But it was a good thing that the fluid did escape; had it gone into the body she would not have lived to tell the story. The swelling having gone down, Jenny returned to the factory. She was not allowed to do any more spinning, and was given another job away from any dust or powder . . . .

Rosina Whyatt, quoted in *Useful Toil*, ed. John Burnett, 1974

Ku Klux Klan: an American racist organisation, whose members wore white robes

Questions

1 What is the writer's attitude to Jenny's illness?

2 What does this suggest about women munition workers' attitude to the risks involved in their jobs?

Assembling wings and tailplanes in an aircraft factory

Factory work was nothing new for women: they had been important in many industries since the Industrial Revolution. But munitions work marked an important advance for women. It showed that they could operate complex machines in dangerous conditions. Although many women did only simple, repetitive tasks, others progressed to setting up and operating sophisticated machine-tools without assistance. This fact, given much publicity in the popular press, helped to convince men of the physical strength and endurance of women, and of the sacrifices they were making to help in the war effort – an important step in the move towards winning the vote and greater social freedom. On a more personal level, too, munitions work marked an improvement for many women: living away from their families, they had a new freedom of movement, and for the first time they had money of their own.

Questions

1   From the information given here, list the jobs carried out by women munition workers. Next to each one, say whether you think it was something traditionally done by women, or something quite new.

2   What different attitudes to women at work are shown in the documents and illustrations in this section? What do these sources tell us about how women were treated in munitions factories? Support your answer with detailed references.

3   You are a munition worker in 1917. A letter has just appeared in your local newspaper saying that 'these munition girls are paid far too much for the simple jobs they do, which require no skill or training'. Write a letter to the paper explaining the work you do and the conditions you work under.

Women in munitions			
	July 1914	July 1915	July 1917	Nov. 1918
Private	210 000	253 000	616 000	700 000
Government	2 000	3 000	203 000	247 000
Total	212 000	256 000	819 000	947 000

4   What proportion of women were working in Government factories in (a) July 1914 and (b) November 1918? What does this suggest about the way in which Government involvement changed during the war?

5   From what you have read in this section, say why there was such a large increase in the number of women employed in munitions factories after July 1915.

How Guy Standish won his VC – the illustration which accompanied the part of the story quoted above right. It appeared in Answers, *a magazine read by lower middle-class men and women*

Nursing and medicine

'We'll never get through, Lucy – but we can die together!' hoarsely shouted Guy Standish as his horse, scorning its double burden, charged gloriously into the band of astonished Uhlans.

Those supreme and thrilling seconds seemed an eternity to Guy, and to the brave but trembling girl whom he was attempting to rescue from a fate worse than death.

G. Edgar: 'A Place in the Sun', *Answers*,
October 1915

Questions

1 What view of the role of women in war, and of their relationship to men, is shown here?

2 Do you think that present-day fiction and television serials still present women nurses in the way they are depicted in the story and illustration above?

At the beginning of the war many women, especially those from middle-class and upper-class backgrounds, were led by a rather romantic view of nursing to volunteer for work in hospitals. They had no idea of the realities they would have to face. In the view of a more down-to-earth volunteer, many such women:

. . . came to the hospital expecting to hold the patients' hands and smooth their pillows while regular nurses fetched and carried everything that looked or smelt disagreeable.

Vera Brittain: *Testament of Youth*, 1933

There were, however, some who foresaw the suffering war would bring, and the demands it would place on nurses. Some years before the war, the Voluntary Aid Detachments and the First Aid Nursing Yeomanry had been formed, and the VADs and FANYs, as they were known, were of vital importance in helping the overworked nurses when fighting began. The first VAD unit left for Boulogne in October 1914, working at first in rest stations and then in military hospitals, where they assisted nurses from the British Red Cross Society and the St John's Ambulance Brigade, and staff from hospitals in England.

In 1915 the Duke of Devonshire opened his London home as a hospital, and soon afterwards wealthy landowners began to offer their country houses for use in the same way. Later that year these houses and several hospitals in England were staffed by the VADs. They worked from 7.30 a.m. to 8 p.m., with three hours off for meals. In theory they had half a day off each week, but in practice the large number of patients often made this impossible. The night shift lasted from eight in the evening to eight in the morning, and was undertaken in two-month stints. For this the volunteers were paid only £20 a year, with a small allowance for uniform and laundry.

For the VADs, many of whom had led sheltered lives and had no knowledge of bodily suffering or hard physical work, the experience was often overwhelming, and many did not stay long. On top of the strain of long hours was the emotional exhaustion of working with men who had suffered terrible wounds and were in constant pain. Enid Bagnold, a VAD who later became a successful novelist, makes this very clear:

> *The man I was to inquire for has no nostrils; they were blown away, and he breathes through two pieces of rubber tubing; it gave a more horrible look to his face than I have ever seen.*
>
> *The Sister came out and told me she thought he was 'not up to much'. I think she means he is dying.*
>
> Enid Bagnold: A Diary Without Dates, 1917

Many of the volunteers lived in hostels, and were away from home for the first time. Most had the further anxiety of having friends or relatives in the forces. For them, life became an exhausting and bewildering routine of work in the wards, from which there was little escape. In another passage from *A Diary Without Dates*, Enid Bagnold sums up the effects of the work:

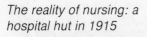

The reality of nursing: a hospital hut in 1915

> *The outside world has faded since I have been in the hospital. Their world is often near me – their mud and trenches, things they say when they come in wounded.*

Mecca: the birthplace of
Mohammed; in this context it
means a favourite or ideal
place

*The worst of it is, it almost bores me to go to London, and
London was always my Mecca. Pity is exhaustible. What a terrible
discovery!*

Questions

1 Why do you think Enid Bagnold is 'almost bored' by going to
London? What does this suggest about her attitude to her work,
and how it has changed her general outlook on life?

2 What does she mean by 'Pity is exhaustible'? Why is this 'a
terrible discovery'?

3 What qualities do you think were needed in a good VAD?

Women did not only work as nurses or assistants in hospitals: many
women doctors did much to ease the suffering of the wounded. Dr
Elsie Inglis, whose offers of help had been rejected so contemp-
tuously by the War Office in 1914, went on to lead a Scottish medical
unit in the Balkans. Two other doctors, Flora Murray and Louisa
Garrett Anderson, founded the Women's Hospital Corps, first at the
Hotel Claridge in Paris, then at Wimereux, and finally in London,
where they worked in a converted workhouse in Endell Street, near
the British Museum. When they arrived they were met by a Colonel
who exclaimed: 'Good God – women!' By the end of the war,
however, they had treated 26 000 patients, with a staff of 180. The
only men were a group of 20 porters whose duties were to lift the
wounded out of the ambulances when they arrived. Work for the
doctors was constant:

*The surgeons spent all their mornings in the wards, and most of their
afternoons in the operating theatre, where it was not unusual to have
a list of twenty or thirty cases on each operating day.*
Flora Murray: *Women as Army Surgeons*, 1920

As well as healing the wounded, Endell Street was important in
developing new medical techniques. It was used, for example, to test
'Bipp'. This was an antiseptic paste which was smeared over wounds
and kept them free of infection for between 10 and 20 days – the
time it often took before surgery was possible, because of the pressure of work at the hospital.

At the end of the war, Sir Alfred Keogh, Director General of
Army Medical Services, wrote to Dr Garrett Anderson, saying: 'I
think your success has probably done more for the cause of women
than anything else I know of.'

How much did the wartime work of women in medicine extend
the opportunities open to women after the war? The work was of
immense value, but it was regarded lightly in some official circles.

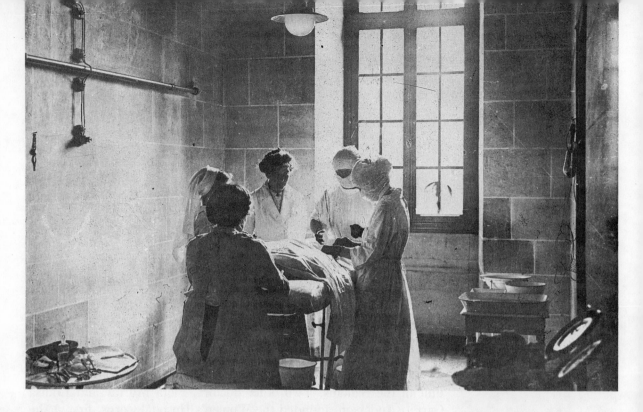

Women surgeons, 1916

Women doctors working overseas, for example, were not paid or graded as officers. The number of women doctors was small, and their work was part of a larger movement in which women were becoming accepted in universities and professions, which had begun many years before the war.

Perhaps the most important long-term effect of women's work in medicine during the war lay in the new liberty of movement which it gave to middle-class women – although they were often too exhausted to make use of it. Here a VAD describes how her life changed:

chaperoned: accompanied by an older woman wherever she went

> *When I was VAD-ing I began in a small country hospital. I was nineteen, very carefully brought up and severely chaperoned. So you may imagine that the war seemed to open a new world to me. I passed suddenly from being the kind of girl I was to being a little person who spent her time in a hospital freeing from lice the uniforms of the soldiers who were brought in! That was my job.*
>
> Mrs C.S. Peel: *How We Lived Then, 1914–1918,* 1929

Questions

1 What do you think was the writer's attitude to her job? How do you think that being a VAD had changed her way of life?

2 You are a surgeon at Endell Street. Write a diary entry for a particularly heavy day in 1918, when the wounded from the last German offensive arrived for treatment.

The services

However far women had taken over men's jobs at home, the idea of women in military uniform as part of the fighting services met with much opposition. Some people felt, as others do today, that women had no place in the armed forces. Others objected that discipline would be hard to maintain; that 'immorality' would result if women were to work closely with men in the forces; or that the work of the voluntary services would be taken over.

Set against these arguments was the pressing need for more people to help with the effort on the various fighting fronts. The move towards women's services could be said to have started when the work of the VADs began to be extended during the second year of war:

The military authorities discovered yet another capacity in which the VAD could serve, and requisitions for cooks and clerks, to release for active service the male orderlies in the hospitals, were received. Thus sprang into existence the general service section of VAD effort, through which were supplied, not only cooks and clerks, but afterwards housemaids, waitresses, ward-orderlies, laundresses, dispensers, X-ray and dental assistants, accountants and telephonists. . . .
The general service section offered, indeed, an opportunity for the woman who was not fitted for nursing, but who yet was able and qualified to undertake some other form of work.

J.A. Hammerton (ed.): *A Popular History of the Great War*, date unknown

By late 1916, with the heavy casualties on the Somme, and growing evidence of women's ability to perform all kinds of war work at home and in the war zone, the pressure was even greater. The work of women ambulance drivers had also shown that women could endure the strain, hardship and danger of working in the battle zone.

In response to these pressures, discussions were held which led to the formation of the Women's Army Auxiliary Corps (WAAC) in July 1917. It had four sections – Clerical, Cookery, Mechanical and Miscellaneous. Its purpose was explained in a book commissioned by the Ministry of Information:

The idea of the WAACs is that they actually replace men. Each cook releases one man, while among the clerks at present the ratio is four women to three men.
Every WAAC who goes to France is like the pawn who attains the top of the chessboard and is exchanged for a more valuable piece. She sends a fighting man to his job by taking all the jobs that are really a woman's after all. For is it not woman's earliest job to look after man?

F. Tennyson Jesse: *The Sword of Deborah*, 1918

The WAACs in France. What impression of the new Corps was this official photograph intended to give?

Questions

1 In the Hammerton passage, what view is presented of women who are unable to work as nurses? Does it suggest that such people are more valuable to the services, or less valuable?

2 What do both the above passages suggest is the main reason for employing women? What does this suggest about the way the services thought of women in comparison with men?

3 Why is it important to the historian to know that *The Sword of Deborah* was commissioned by the Ministry of Information?

The work done by a WAAC varied according to the section in which she was employed. She might carry out tasks traditionally seen as 'women's work' – cooking, cleaning, sewing, or waiting on soldiers in the Officers' Club. Alternatively, she might take on more 'masculine' roles, such as driving 3-ton lorries in the Motor Transport Section; this was heavy, dangerous work, travelling along roads pitted by shell-holes in vehicles that were difficult to steer and control. She might also be involved in erecting buildings or working as a carpenter's labourer at a base area.

Forty-one thousand women served in the WAACs, 17 000 of them overseas. Yet although they were part of the armed forces, they had no military ranks, since by tradition the King's Commission could be given only to men. Instead of officers and sergeants, there were 'controllers', 'administrators' and 'forewomen'.

The WAACs were followed by the Women's Royal Naval Service, known as the 'Wrens', and the WRAF, or Women's Royal Air

Women carpenters in the
WAACs erecting a workshop
building

Force. Many women were employed as clerks or typists, but others
became mechanics and motorcycle dispatch riders. In 1918, the work
done by the women's services was recognised by royal approval: the
WAACs became the Queen Mary's Army Auxiliary Corps.

Questions

1   Do you think that the work done by women in the services
    offered them greater independence, or the prospect of new
    kinds of employment in civilian life? Support your answer with
    examples chosen from the jobs described.

2   How do the attitudes towards women shown in this section
    compare with present-day views on the role of women? Which
    attitudes have changed, and which have remained the same?

3   You are a new recruit to the WAACs in 1917. Write a letter to
    your sister at home telling her about your work.

The police

The services were not the only organisations in which women wore
military-style uniforms, as the war also saw the beginning of the
Women's Police Service. Early in the war, many middle-class women
were concerned about moral standards. Large army camps were the
scene of 'provocative loitering' by some women and girls, and the
London railway stations, where trains bringing soldiers home on

Members of the Women's Police Service

leave arrived at frequent intervals, became the haunts of prostitutes. The larger number of women working also meant that children and young people generally had less supervision.

In the first year of the war women university graduates, and others from what was known as 'a good background', formed Voluntary Patrols. At the same time, Margaret Dawson formed the Women Police Volunteers.

During her 12-hour patrol shift, a volunteer policewoman would encounter all kinds of problems. She might deal with couples engaging in 'public immorality' in parks or shop doorways; she might intervene in a domestic quarrel involving young children; or, if an air raid occurred (they were less frequent but no less frightening than those in World War II), she would have to shepherd anxious people to whatever shelter was available, and try to prevent looting and theft. A frequent task was to try to clear prostitutes from residential areas. A letter from a London vicar after a campaign of this sort shows the success of the women police:

> *Most of the women have disappeared from the neighbourhood, and the rest reformed. With regard to the soldiers, who were mostly overseas men, good work has been done, and many were deeply grateful for the warning given them. I would strongly recommend any brother faced with a similar state of things to apply to the Women's Police Service.*

> Quoted in David Mitchell's book,
> *Women on the Warpath*, 1966

The policewomen were not only active against vice. In 1915 the organisation, now called the Women's Police Service, agreed to carry out duties for the Ministry of Munitions. These included patrolling railway stations in areas where there were munitions factories, searching women workers for dangerous objects, and settling disagreements and disturbances in and around the factories.

In 1916 it became possible for women to be paid from the local police fund, and by the end of the war London, Manchester, Hull and 26 other towns and one county were employing policewomen. About half the total force were 'educated' or 'professional' women. This could be a handicap in certain places, and for some duties, but in general the policewomen were respected by those with whom they dealt. They made an important contribution to changing the way women were thought of in society, and in extending the opportunities available to them.

Questions

1 Look again at the vicar's letter. What was his attitude to (a) prostitution and (b) policewomen? Do you think this source attributes blame equally to the prostitutes and their clients?

2 From what you have read, do you think that women police constables were treated as equals of the men they worked with, for example in the duties they performed? Give reasons for your answer.

Women in business

In the years before the war, women had begun to take over the male-dominated world of the clerk, by becoming what were then known as 'typewriters'. The great shortage of manpower at home, and the great expansion of Government offices caused by the war, meant that there was a desperate need for women who could type or carry out other clerical tasks. How desperate the need was is shown by one woman's recollection of how she found a job 'in a wholly male chartered accountants' office in the City':

> When I arrived for an interview I was somewhat taken aback to find a number of other applicants waiting to be interviewed, and when my turn came to appear before the Senior Partner, I began by remarking that I was afraid I should be of no use to the Firm, and when he asked my reason, I replied that it was literally the very first time I had ever been inside an office. I had never even been into my home town solicitors' office. Despite which ... I was asked the earliest date I could start work.
>
> Mrs G.M. Pearson: recollections in the
> Peter H. Liddle 1914–18 Personal Experience Archives,
> Sunderland Polytechnic

Questions

1   What does this passage suggest about the number of women
    who wanted to work in offices at this time?

2   How would you describe the way in which Mrs Pearson
    approached her interview? Does this suggest anything about
    the way in which women were regarded by business concerns
    at this time?

Towns and cities throughout the country saw the emergence of a new
kind of woman, who travelled by train or bus to a Government or
commercial office, ate alone at a Lyons Corner House at lunch time,
and often visited restaurants and theatres without a male escort in
the evening. For the first time, many such women had economic
independence. A reliable shorthand typist could command up to 35
shillings (£1.75) a week even in 1915. This was a good wage and,
although transport and food were costly, many women began to live
at a much higher standard because of their new commercial careers.

For middle-class women such work offered the hope of a professional career; for the working classes, it was an appealing alter-
native to domestic service. By the end of the war, nearly one million
women were employed in commerce – nearly twice the figure for
1914. Once again, a movement begun before the war had become
firmly established, and the new breed of commuting women was here
to stay; there could be no return to the kitchen and the scullery for
these women after the war.

Below left: *women working
in the Food Control Office*

Transport

Working on the railways, buses and trams had always been a male preserve, but the war did much to extend the work of women in the transport industry. In the following passage a historian sums up their contribution:

> *In public transport systems – on the omnibuses, trams, tubes and trains, women replaced men employees in large numbers. They were taken on in thousands, in fact, and on the Underground, District, Tube, and other railways, acted as lift operators, ticket collectors, and gate-women on the trains. Some were porters, others travelling ticket inspectors, and clerks in the booking-office. The London General Omnibus Company employed about 2,100 women on omnibuses as conductors and time-keepers at points. During the air raids those employed on omnibuses behaved very well in the face of danger, and the same may be said of those who worked on the Tubes, where the dense crowds that assembled made their work very trying.*
>
> J.A. Hammerton (ed.): *A Popular History of the Great War*, date unknown

There was resistance at first to employing women to drive trams and buses, but the need became more urgent after the introduction of conscription in January 1916, when men were called up for compulsory military service. Wealthier women had been driving cars before the war; now women of all classes wanted to acquire this skill, and instruction was provided by garages and Government training schools. By 1916, all the London ambulances were driven by women – tiring work in the days before synchromesh and power steering. Transport of all kinds saw the largest increase in the employment of women in any industry in the war years. Unlike commerce, however, this was to be only a temporary change. It was not until World War II that women bus conductors again became commonplace; and even today a woman driving a heavy truck, bus or train is an unusual sight.

Below: volunteer drivers under instruction, 1916

Agriculture

By the harvest of 1915, many farmers were facing difficulties in finding labourers, but instead of employing women they recruited schoolboys, students and even prisoners of war. The reasons for their reluctance have been explained by a modern historian:

> *As a rule, before the war women did not work with horses, sheep, or beef cattle, and field work was regarded in many areas as degrading.... Moreover, men working in the fields did not want*

bavers: tea break

women with them to inhibit the masculine conversations at 'bavers' and dinner-time; they judged that much of the field-work, extending over ten or eleven hours daily, was beyond the physical strength of most women, nor could they shift the four-bushel sacks of seed for the drills, or of grain from the threshers.

Edith Whetham: *The Agrarian History of England and Wales, Vol. VIII; 1914–1939,* 1978

Many people, however, felt that women could do useful work on farms. Women organised competitions to show their skill, and one judge found that 'some of the work was very well done indeed', although he still felt that 'the heavy work on a farm must be done by men'.

Gradually resistance was overcome, and some women began working on farms. However, it was not until 1917, when the German submarine campaign made the demand for home-grown food acute, that the Women's Land Army was formed.

The Land Army had three branches – agriculture, timber-cutting and forage (looking after foodstuffs for army horses). The women were paid 18 shillings (90p) a week – more than the pre-war male farmworker's 14 shillings (70p), but less than the wages earned by women in munitions or commerce. After a month's training, they moved to the farms and were billeted with families or lived in hostels.

A magazine called *The Landswoman*, produced by and for Land Army women, appeared in January 1918. Its first issue contained this passage:

Women working on an elevating machine

Hard manual labour, rough feeding and their own special dis-
comforts of housing and housekeeping are the lot of women on the
land. But those who toil with the men, sharing their field life, living
on less than their wages, cease to be 'foreigners' to the villagers . . .
women's physical endurance and manual labour have earned the
respect of the villagers, disarmed their suspicions, are breaking down
their reserve and winning their confidence.

Farm work was hard – and lonely, too, for women used to city life.
Land Army women earned less than most women war-workers, and
their work lacked glamour; but they contributed much to the
nation's economic survival in the last 18 months of the war.

Questions

1   What objections did farmers raise to the employment of women
on the land? Do you think that any of these objections were
based on fact rather than prejudice?

2   Do you think that the passage from *The Landswoman* paints an
accurate picture of life on the land? Use words and phrases
from the article to support your answer.

3   What factors might have influenced the way the writer saw the
work of the Land Army?

Other occupations

Women also worked in a range of other jobs which had previously
been done only by men.

As we have seen, many took over the family business when their
husbands went off to fight, working as chimney sweeps or black-
smiths, operating printing presses or running bakeries. Here is a
contemporary response to the situation:

'For men must work and women must weep' does not illustrate the
attitude of modern Woman to the affairs of the world. . . . To-day's
woman is essentially a comrade to man, and a helper; also, she has
ably proved that she can do her share in times of crises.

The War Illustrated, 24 April 1915

The list of occupations that women took on in the later stages of the
war is long and varied. It ranges from delivering the mail in remote
country districts to excavating shipyard basins in the north; from
digging graves to training as pharmacists; from working as waitresses
in men's clubs to loading trucks in lime quarries.

Several of these jobs were short-term ventures, taken on by
women to free more men for the fighting. Some were voluntary

Barges of salvage – waste metal from the front – being unloaded by women. What are the men in uniform doing?

activities for the wealthy. But there were others which represented more permanent steps towards equality of opportunity with men. The advances were not always what they seemed, however. Some jobs were taken over so completely that they came to be seen as 'women's work', and were poorly paid as a result. How far the genuine advances were maintained is the subject of the next chapter.

Women in employment during the war		
	1914	*1918*
Transport	18 200	117 200
Buses	300	4 300
Trams	1 200	18 800
Railways	12 000	65 000
Other (private)	200	5 800
Business	505 200	934 500
Farming	190 000	228 000
Industry	2 178 600	2 970 600
National and Local Government (including teaching)	262 200	460 000
Domestic service	1 658 000	1 250 000
Professions, nurses, secretaries, typists and other home workers	542 000	652 500
Entertainment and hotels	181 000	220 000
In own businesses	430 000	470 000
Total in employment	5 966 000	7 311 000
Total women	23 721 000	24 538 000

Women navvies excavating a wet basin for a shipbuilding yard (1918 caption). Why do you think the men are using a mechanical excavator while the women are using shovels?

Questions

1   Make a list of war jobs for women, separating them into groups according to their long-term effects. Judging from what you have read so far, divide them into the following categories:
    a) Temporary jobs to free men for the fighting.
    b) Voluntary tasks which would finish when the war ended.
    c) New areas which would later become 'women's work'.
    d) Areas which were genuine advances in opportunity.

2   In which occupations did the largest increase in the employment of women occur?

3   In which field did the employment of women decrease? Give reasons for your answer.

4   You live in a country area but pay a visit to a large town by train in the autumn of 1918. Write a letter to a friend at home telling her about the various jobs you have seen women doing during your journey, and give your own opinions about how the war will change women's lives.

Recollections

The following passages are women war workers' recollections, taken from the Peter Liddle 1914–1918 Personal Experience Archives at Sunderland Polytechnic. They offer further insights into the working lives of women during World War I.

Gladys Robson was employed at the Armstrong Whitworth munition works at Scotwood. She became involved in trade union activities, and later went on to be a Justice of the Peace.

I remember the strike in 1916 when all the shops (shell shop, fuse shops) came out on strike for more money. We, the delegates, were called into the manager's office and were told we would go to prison if we did not get the women back to work, as it was illegal to strike in wartime. 8,000 women stopped work. We telephoned the union in London to come to our aid and I was selected to go to the Central Station to meet (we thought Margaret Bondfield) but Susan Lawrence came instead. They asked me to wear my badge in my coat to identify myself. I met her and took her to the management. The strike was over that day, and we got the money we were entitled to and back pay that day.

Norah S. Bristow worked at the War Office:

I got the chance through a family friend in HM Office of Works, of going, after being very much vetted, into the War Office, to start in the new department dealing with the issuing of army pensions. This was now beginning to get busy as casualties came in, and for which women were being recruited for the first time on the staff. We started working in a small room in the War Office. I was No. 12 as far as I can remember and gradually as the work grew we were transferred to huts in St James's Park. Then as Widows' Pensions became more numerous they were separated into another office. By 1916, when an increase in casualties brought a corresponding increase in the work of issuing the pensions, and in the number of clerks, a huge 4-storeyed building in Baker St W1 was taken over.... I became a section head with about 30 women of all ages under me and we were certainly very busy and life was very hectic with the overtime and travelling into London each day, coping with the blackout out of doors and in the buildings with such quantities of staff.

Mrs Claire Mitchell had worked before the war making 'Field Service Cables', earning 8 shillings (40p) a week. Seeking a higher wage, she applied to an industrial plant at Trafford Park.

I was lucky and given a job as an electric crane driver. To get into the plant I had to wear my badge which I still have, we had to memorise the number and be able to give it to the guard if questioned. We had to work from 6 a.m. to 6 p.m. for two weeks on 'days' and then 6 p.m. to 6 a.m. on 'nights' also for two weeks. The cranes were carrying tons of steel bars which my slingers selected and then put on the carrier, which was electrified, across 5 bars. I then switched on and carried them to a machine where they were cut into pieces to make large shells. This was also piece-work but on a much higher scale and I never collected less than £12 a week.

Questions

1   Does the figure of £12 a week as a wage seem accurate, in comparison with the wages mentioned elsewhere in this chapter? Does this suggest that recollections might present difficulties for the historian? Can you find similar points in the other passages?

2   What other difficulties do recollections present to someone looking for factual information about women's war work?

3   What do you think are the most important kinds of information that recollections can offer to the historian? Give an example of each kind from these three passages.

3

CHANGE AT HOME AND WORK

Food and the family

The bread during the war was very poor, of a dirty colour. It was not refined at all – everything was ground in – yet it was not brown bread ... the children would stand outside the school gates where the soldiers were billeted waiting for any leftovers which they took home to their mothers, sometimes whole loaves of bread.

Miss W. Liddle: recollections in the Peter H. Liddle 1914–18
Personal Experience Archives, Sunderland Polytechnic

Children outside a factory asking for scraps of bread

This passage shows very clearly the shortage of basic foodstuffs during the war, which women had somehow to overcome. In January 1917, the Germans declared unrestricted submarine warfare, and a vast tonnage of ships bringing food from America, Canada and what was then the British Empire was lost. In May, the country had enough grain to last only nine weeks. The King issued a proclamation urging families to 'reduce the consumption of bread ... by at least one-fourth', and the Ministry of Food issued a leaflet about how to save 'Mr Slice o'Bread'. Shortages of grain forced the price of a 41b loaf up from its pre-war 4½d. (2p) to 11½d. (4½p). A Government subsidy of £60 million brought the price down to 9d. (3½p) for the whole of the following year.

The shortage of bread is only one example of the lack of food in the war years. The price of items that were in heavy demand rose steeply. Eggs had been 1s.3d. (6p) a dozen in 1914; in 1918, they were 6s.3d. (31p). Sugar was three and a half times its 1914 price by 1918, and the price of imported beef had trebled. Butter was often almost impossible to find in the shops, and when it was available it was so expensive that it was beyond the reach of most shoppers. The Ministry of Food took over production of margarine in 1917; even so, at 1s.2d. a pound in 1918 it was still twice its pre-war price.

Wages had risen, of course – in general by two or two and a half times their 1914 levels – and many women who had not had jobs before the war found themselves unexpectedly better off. Those with large families, however, found it hard to manage and, then as now, inflation affected the poor most of all. The Ministry of Food offered advice on how to manage:

The first step towards the saving of food in the home is that the housewife should attend herself to every detail. If any part of the household management be left to others, whether shopping, the arrangement of meals, or the methods of cooking, there will, as a rule, be waste. Every penny spent should, of course, be put down and week compared with week.

Edmund I. Spriggs MD FRCP: *Food and How to Save it,* Ministry of Food, 1918

Questions

1 What view of the nature of the 'housewife's' duties is shown in the extract above? What role is she expected to play in the fight against food shortages?

2 Given the number of women heavily involved in war work in 1918, does it strike you as odd that the 'housewife' should be advised to 'attend herself to every detail'? How well do you think the writer knew the people he was writing for?

3 In what ways do you think the general view of 'housewives' is different today? Think, in particular, about the ways in which food and household products are advertised.

Average weekly wages of women and girls in all industries

1906 (Wage census)	12s.8d.	(64p)
1915 (December)	14s.10d.	(74½p)
1916 (December)	16s.8d.	(84p)
1917 (December)	20s.5d.	(£1.02)
1918 (November)	25s.4d.	(£1.26½p)

4 By what proportion did wages rise between 1906 and 1915?

5 By what proportion did they rise between 1915 and 1918?

6 What does the difference in the rate of increase suggest about the effect of the war upon earnings?

Official rationing of food – and some other items, such as coal – had begun in some parts of the country in 1917, but in 1918 a national scheme was announced. It meant that, as well as stretching their housekeeping money to cover the cost of food, women with families, like everyone else, had to register with shops and plan the week's meals around the 'coupons' – tiny pieces of paper in the ration book which entitled its owner to small amounts of meat or other precious foods. Yet despite the shortages, general standards of health rose during the war, as did the average life expectancy. Modern historians put this down to the number of people, especially women, who were earning for the first time in their lives; the extra income raised the living standard of many of the poorer families.

Overcoming the shortages was almost entirely the responsibility of women. It was certainly nothing new for the wife and mother – especially in poorer families – to have to save every penny and seize

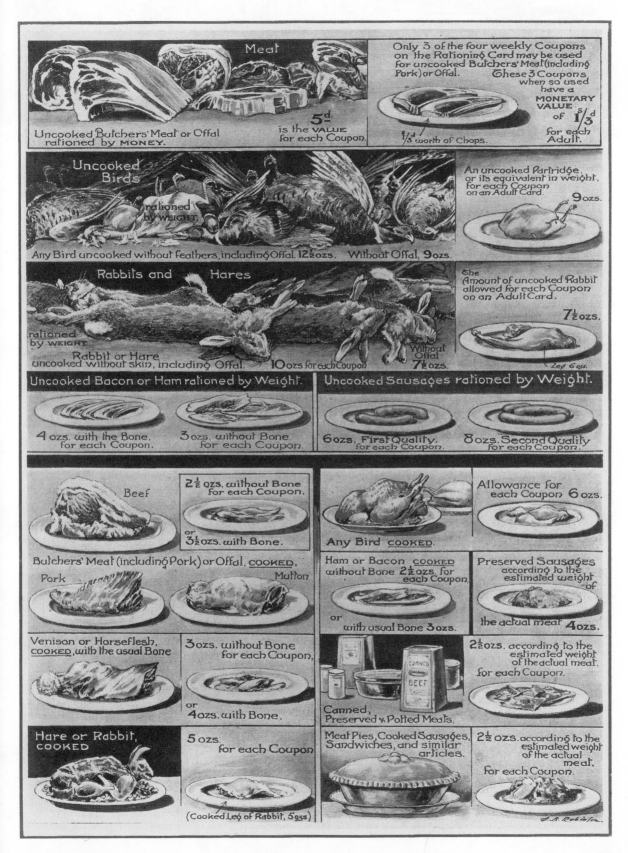

Meat

Uncooked Butchers' Meat or Offal rationed by MONEY.

5d. is the VALUE for each Coupon.

Only 3 of the four weekly Coupons on the Rationing Card may be used for uncooked Butchers' Meat (including Pork) or Offal. These 3 Coupons when so used have a MONETARY VALUE of 1/3 for each Adult.

1/3 worth of Chops.

Uncooked Birds rationed by WEIGHT

Any Bird uncooked without feathers, including Offal, 12½ ozs. Without Offal, 9 ozs.

An uncooked Partridge, or its equivalent in weight, for each Coupon on an Adult Card. 9 ozs.

Rabbits and Hares rationed by WEIGHT

Rabbit or Hare uncooked without skin, including Offal, 10 ozs. for each Coupon. Without Offal, 7½ ozs.

The Amount of uncooked Rabbit allowed for each Coupon on an Adult Card. 7½ ozs.

Leg 6 ozs.

Uncooked Bacon or Ham rationed by Weight.

4 ozs. with the Bone, for each Coupon.

3 ozs. without Bone, for each Coupon.

Uncooked Sausages rationed by Weight.

6 ozs. First Quality, for each Coupon.

8 ozs. Second Quality for each Coupon.

Beef

2½ ozs. without Bone for each Coupon, or 3½ ozs. with Bone.

Butchers' Meat (including Pork) or Offal, COOKED.

Pork

Mutton

Any Bird COOKED.

Allowance for each Coupon 6 ozs.

Ham or Bacon COOKED without Bone 2½ ozs. for each Coupon, or with usual Bone 3 ozs.

Preserved Sausages according to the estimated weight of the actual meat 4 ozs.

Venison or Horseflesh, COOKED, with the usual Bone

3 ozs. without Bone for each Coupon, or 4 ozs. with Bone.

Canned, Preserved or Potted Meats.

CORNED BEEF

2½ ozs. according to the estimated weight of the actual meat, for each Coupon.

Hare or Rabbit, COOKED

5 ozs. for each Coupon

(Cooked Leg of Rabbit, 5 ozs.)

Meat Pies, Cooked Sausages, Sandwiches, and similar articles.

2½ ozs. according to the estimated weight of the actual meat, for each Coupon.

F. S. Robinson.

39

Women buying vegetables in 1917. What does this picture tell the historian about shopping and eating habits and the style of dress at this time?

every chance to provide enough food for the household, but the war made this need far greater, and added further to the burdens faced by women with families.

By the height of the war, the average wife and mother faced and overcame great difficulties. She had to clothe and feed the children, managing in spite of shortages to make sure that there was enough, or nearly enough, to eat. She had to see that adult members of the family on heavy manual work – which might well include herself – had a suitable diet for their jobs. In many parts of the country, she had also to endure air raids, and the drab, colourless life of a nation that had been at war for several years. Yet somehow she had to keep going, binding the family together in the face of general worries about the war and anxieties about the safety of a husband, father or brother away fighting. And all this often came on top of war work in a factory – in many cases done at night so that she might snatch more time to look after the family by day.

The effects of this strain were noted in an official report:

> *Where home conditions are bad, as they frequently are, where a long working day is aggravated by long hours of travelling and where, in addition, housing accommodation is inadequate, family life is defaced beyond recognition. . . . A day begun at 4 or even 3.30 a.m., for work at 6 a.m., followed by 14 hours in the factory and another 2 or 2½ hours on the journey back, may end at 10 or 10.30 p.m., in a home or lodging where the prevailing degree of overcrowding precludes any possibility of comfortable rest. In such conditions of confusion, pressure and overcrowding, home can have no existence.*
>
> Great Britain Ministry of Munitions, Health of Munition Workers Committee, *Memorandum No 4*, 'Employment of Women'

It is 1917. You are a woman of 28, with a daughter of ten, a son of eight and twin boys aged four and a half. Your husband is fighting in France, and you work in a factory making aircraft parts. Write a letter to your sister in Australia telling her what life is like for you.

The pressures described here did not apply to all women. Those with families fared worst; during the war it seemed that the old saying that a working woman has two jobs to do was more true than ever. This meant that, after the war, although many single women wished to continue working, to extend the freedom they had enjoyed as wage earners, many married women wanted to go back to the traditional role of wife and mother. In this way, some of the advances won by working women during the war were lost.

After the war

Strain and hardship were not the only effects of the war upon working women. There were also more positive changes in habits and standards. Perhaps most important was the change in outlook in women who, at last, were being taken seriously as working people in their own right. This was most true of young, single women, but something of this new power and self-respect was probably felt by every woman who worked. The following passage sums up the effects of this new mood:

> *War work, with good wages, has not only taught women the comfort and luxury of earned money, and raised their standard of the necessities of life – it has not only proved their power as workers for the community, but it has given them a hunger for work as well.*
> Grace Curnock: 'Demobilising the Women; finding work for a
> Million,' *The War Illustrated*, 18 January 1919

Questions

1 Do you think that the writer is being completely accurate when she speaks of the 'comfort and luxury of earned money'? Discuss what this phrase means, and whether or not it applied to all women workers.

2 What does the title of this article tell you about the author's ideas of the role of women after the war?

For several generations working-class women had been going out to work, so the changes caused by the war were far greater for middle-class women, in particular the unmarried daughters. Instead of being confined to the family home, often as unpaid servants for their fathers or brothers, and being accompanied by elderly aunts on social outings, they had carried out difficult or dangerous jobs far from home and had moved freely and on their own in public. All this created a desire for even more freedom of opportunity in the years after the Armistice. The right to vote was one way in which this would be satisfied, as the next chapter shows. But to what extent would the hunger for greater opportunity and social freedom be satisfied in the post-war years?

At first, it seemed that there would be real progress. On leaving war jobs in 1919, women were given a 'donation' of 25 shillings (£1.25) a week, for 13 weeks, which was supposed to tide them over until they found civilian work. This suggested that the Government would treat them as near equals with men in paying unemployment benefit and pensions – even though the rates were far below those given to demobilised servicemen.

More jobs were becoming open to women, too. The Sex Disqualification (Removal) Act of 1919 provided that:

> *A person shall not be disqualified by sex or marriage from the exercise of any public function, or from being appointed to or holding any civil or judicial office or post, from entering or assuming or carrying on any civil profession or vocation.*

In 1920, Oxford University agreed to award degrees to women. In the following year, women were allowed to become barristers, and to sit on juries. The census carried out in the same year revealed the number of women in the professions; there were 1 253 doctors, 49 architects, 20 barristers, 17 solicitors and 46 consultant engineers – figures up to seven times their pre-war equivalents in the cases where there had been any women at all in the professions before the war. For those with less extensive training, new jobs were available in electrical goods factories, and in offices. It seemed that, with the post-war boom in trade, building and commerce, new possibilities were becoming increasingly available for women of all backgrounds.

Progress was not restricted to the field of work – social freedom also continued to grow. 'Flappers', young women mainly from upper-class backgrounds, shocked their elders by smoking, drinking, raising their hemlines and having their hair cut short. The wartime liberty to attend theatres and restaurants without male escorts was now taken for granted. All this soon filtered down to the office girls and factory workers, with the help of mass-produced, fashionable clothes and the growth of popular women's magazines.

These social changes were positive and permanent; the new freedom has never been lost. But in terms of employment and career prospects, the picture soon became more gloomy:

> *The women who only a year or so earlier had been acclaimed as patriots, giving up easy lives at home to work for their Country in*

her hour of need, were now represented as vampires who deprived men of their rightful jobs. By Trade Union pressure they were dismissed from engineering, printing, and transport work, though cheap and efficient workers, and from the factories where they had worked on munitions. No Unemployment Benefit scheme was arranged for them.

Robert Graves and Alan Hodge: *The Long Weekend; A Social History of Great Britain 1918–1939*, 1940

Questions

1 How would you describe the tone of this passage? For example, is it serious or comic? Do the authors think women were treated fairly after the war?

2 Do you think that the Act of Parliament of 1919 actually encouraged women to enter new professions? Think carefully about the way in which it is worded, and also about the number of women in professions, as shown in the 1921 census.

Fashions can often tell us a lot about how people feel and behave. Left: *fashions in 1914.* Below: *fashions in 1925. What are the main differences? What changes do they suggest in the social position and role of women?*

The dismissal of women, which began with the return of men from the forces, continued with the 'slump' or economic depression of the middle and late twenties. Many people felt that it was wrong to pay women the same wage as a man who had a family to support. Unless they could afford an education beyond the school-leaving age of 14, and perhaps enter a profession, women wanting work often had to go back into the drudgery of domestic service, from which the war had released so many. Just after the war there was an acute shortage of servants, as so many women were still on war work. As they were dismissed, however, many went into service, and numbers employed in this area rose by 200 000 in the twenties. Their conditions were very different from those experienced by women war workers:

Though a resident servant was not expected to work all day without stopping she often had to be available for work all day, and had no definite hours off duty except, perhaps, a Sunday afternoon every fortnight and one evening a week. Girls working in a factory, shop or office could do what they liked with their Sundays and spare evenings; moreover, they usually worked alongside others of their own age. The young girl in service often had no such companionship, and her opportunities of meeting the opposite sex were much reduced, and with them the chances of marrying.

Noreen Branson: *Britain in the Nineteen Twenties*, 1975

Questions

1 Compare the life of a woman in domestic service with some of the accounts of women in war work given in Chapter 2. Think

about the good and bad points of each, and decide which you think you would prefer to have done.

2 Construct a balance sheet of achievements for women in the twenties, listing the good and the bad points.

Employment prospects changed little for most women in the thirties. New jobs did arise in some areas, however, because of the development of new products. Many women worked in the 'trim shops' of car factories, making upholstery and carpets for the new mass-produced cars such as the Morris 8 and Austin 7, but they had no real job security and were laid off when sales of cars fell. Other women worked in electrical factories, making radio receivers. The conditions of work in both kinds of factory owed much to advances made in the wartime munitions works, but life was easier for the workers as there was less pressure. Workers in the trim shop at Cowley, for example, sat at long tables sewing seat-covers, singing the latest hit songs to make the time pass more quickly.

Through most of the thirties, unemployment was high. Few new jobs were open to women: the main areas were secretarial work – by now traditionally 'women's work', and therefore poorly paid – and factory work. At the other end of the scale there were the professions, open only to a tiny minority. It seemed that work in the home was once again the dominant occupation for women, either in domestic service or as a housewife and mother. True, the life of the average woman at home was made easier by the development of gas

Below left: women typists at the Milk Marketing Board, 1934

cookers, electric irons, and really new machines called vacuum cleaners; but this was poor consolation for someone who needed a job or wanted a career.

Finding employment was made more difficult by the fact that many people felt that married women should not work. Many employers dismissed women when they married. Married women teachers, for example, were very rare indeed at this time.

All this changed with the coming of war in 1939. Work on munitions, especially aircraft manufacture, had expanded rapidly since the Munich crisis of 1938, and women formed up to 90 per cent of the workforce in some factories. Early volunteers were classified as 'mobile' unless they had husbands in the forces; they were moved to factories throughout the country, either staying with families or living in hostels. War work had been voluntary throughout the 1914–18 war, but conscription was introduced in 1941 for unmarried women and childless widows between the ages of 19 and 30. Women who were 'called up' were put either into the services or into the factories. In 1942 all women up to the age of 45 were interviewed. The following year the 'Grannies call-up', of women aged 45–60, was begun, but few were drafted because of public protest.

The kind of work done by women during World War II is summed up in the following passage:

> *A Blackpool dress-shop worker directed in 1942 into the local Vickers Armstrong factory, where she helped to sew the fabric on to the wings of Wellington bombers, remembers how when the output was stepped up to a wing a day, this meant sewing seventy feet of Irish linen, specially treated to make it hard, at eight painful stitches to the inch. . . . Perhaps the most unpleasant, and certainly the most dangerous, work of all was in the bomb and shell filling factories. For safety reasons, plants handling explosives had to be isolated and the individual buildings dispersed, often meaning two or three hours a day spent in travelling and a long walk on the site. The chemicals, too, could have unpleasant side-effects, and one woman . . . found that not merely her hands but the soles of her feet turned bright yellow.*
>
> Norman Longmate: *How We Lived Then*, 1971

Below: *women conscripted into munition factories in World War II, 1939–45*

Question

From the above passage and the illustration on page 18, work out the similarities and differences between working conditions in munition work in World War I and World War II. What changes had been made to improve working conditions and safety standards? What do you conclude from these changes about the general attitude towards the employment of women in World War II?

After the war, the bleak economic conditions of the forties, which produced the 'Export or Die' campaign, and the 'affluent society' of the fifties, ensured that many women stayed in work – a situation that hardly changed until the depression of the late seventies.

The position of women today is full of contradictions. Legally, nothing stands in the way of women being employed on an equal footing with men, and in equal numbers. The Equal Opportunities Commission has been set up to protect women's rights, the feminist lobby is powerful, and legislation covers areas such as maternity leave and sex discrimination. Reliable contraception has meant that women can decide whether or not to have children – although pressures from society or their male partners often mean that they are not free to take this decision for themselves. Socially, women today have far greater freedom and opportunities than the campaigners of 1914 would have thought possible.

Yet still, in many ways, women seem to be 'second class citizens'. In times of high unemployment, women find it hard to obtain work, regardless of their qualifications, and many have fallen back on part-time work and the jobs which have become the new 'women's work' – operating supermarket check-outs and entering data into VDUs. A report published in 1986 revealed cases of women outworkers – people who work in their own homes – being paid between 11p and 16p an hour. There are many women in important, highly paid jobs; yet there are also many whose talents and skills remain unfulfilled. Perhaps it is too early for us to see things clearly: a future historian will have to decide how far the advances won by women in World War I were maintained and extended in the 1980s.

Questions

1 Talk to some working women. Find out what they do, and the conditions they work in; the length of their working day, and the amount they are paid; the laws which protect them at work, and the holidays (if any) they are entitled to.

2 Working in small groups and sharing the data you have collected, discuss the number and nature of the changes in work since World War I. How different are things now? Draw up a table like the one below, putting ticks in the appropriate columns for each aspect of work.

	Better	Worse	The same
Working conditions			
Length of day			
Pay			
Laws			
Holidays			

4

WOMEN AND POLITICS

Voices of dissent

I could not give my name to aid the slaughter in this war, fought on both sides for grossly material ends, which did not justify the sacrifice of a single mother's son. Clearly I must continue to oppose it, and expose it, to all whom I could reach with voice or pen. Clearly I must declare that the 'National Service' in industry the Government was proposing, was not the collective action of a free people agreeing on equal terms to subordinate their individual ends for the common weal, but the enslavement of the many for the profit of the few.

Sylvia Pankhurst: *The Home Front*, 1932

the common weal: the good of all

These words, written by one of the leading campaigners for reform before World War I, remind us of an important truth. Although the overwhelming majority of women supported the war, becoming involved in whatever way they could, there was still a significant minority who opposed it.

Many felt the war was wrong because they thought it was being fought for material gain, with companies and individuals making vast 'war profits' by exploiting working people, aided by a Government which apparently did little to protect the workers' interests. In this area of opposition, Sylvia Pankhurst was prominent. She campaigned tirelessly for equal pay for women war workers, writing letters and sending petitions to Lloyd George. She met pensioners and discussed their plight when food and other costs were soaring. She helped women appearing before Munitions Tribunals – bodies which decided whether workers could change from one employer to another – and, in her paper *The Workers' Dreadnought*, made public the names of companies who exploited female labour, under headings such as 'Records of Disgraceful Sweating'. All in all, she and her supporters were a thorn in the flesh of the authorities, and she achieved a good deal in lessening hardship in many individual cases.

Protests at the price of milk, 1916

Question

Do you think Sylvia Pankhurst was against the war only because it allowed employers to make large profits? What other reasons for her opposition do you think are suggested in the extract from her book?

Other women campaigned against the war on moral or religious grounds. When conscription was introduced in 1916, men who opposed the war could appeal to a tribunal as conscientious objec-

Hettie Wheeldon, Winnie Mason and Mrs Alice Wheeldon guarded by a wardress while awaiting trial for attempting to murder Lloyd George with poison darts in 1917. There was little evidence, yet Mrs Wheeldon was sentenced to 10 years' penal servitude. She helped 'conchies' and deserters. Does this tell you anything about public attitudes to those who opposed the war?

tors. Some young women, seeing a man out of uniform in the street, would press a white feather into his hand as a badge of cowardice; but others, led by Catherine Marshall, became involved in the No-Conscription Fellowship, an organisation which tried to protect the 'conchies' from the unjust and often brutal treatment they received. An idea of how strongly such people felt is given in a letter written by a Cambridge undergraduate in 1916:

> *God's curse on our ancestors who have driven half our generation to hell and death and the other half to slavery and despair. And three times cursed be the old who sit here telling us young ones 'our duty', and occasionally deigning to praise the nobleness of those who are defending their precious skins and property. It would have made you sick to see the tribunals – 7 aged fat old men explaining to nervous young ones the sacred duty of defending them.*
>
> *The Conscientious Objectors ... are the only people with a spark of spirit left and, by Heaven, they are holding out splendidly.*
>
> Helen Wedgewood: a letter to her father, quoted in Peter H. Liddle's book, *Aspects of Conflict 1916*, 1985, from the original in the Peter H. Liddle 1914–18 Personal Experience Archives, Sunderland Polytechnic

---

Questions

1 Look again at the letter. At which particular group of people is the writer's anger directed? Does the letter suggest what the writer felt was the cause of the war and its suffering?

2 Think about the number of women involved in war work, as shown in the tables in Chapter 2, and the large numbers who had relatives involved in the fighting. With this in mind, decide whether the views expressed in Helen Wedgewood's letter were held by the majority of women at the time.

The tradition of women against war continued through the 1930s to today's peace movement, with its demonstrations at Greenham Common and elsewhere. Here, a women's peace demonstration marches through Trafalgar Square in 1936. Compare this picture with those on page 8. What do the differences suggest about how women, and their approach to politics, had changed over the years?

Some women based their opposition on more practical grounds, such as the rise in the price of milk or the general level of wartime inflation. Perhaps feelings of this kind were the nearest that very many women came to voicing protest at the war and the way it was being conducted.

Others felt discontent at a rather deeper level.

Many women, perhaps most women, are still caught in the meshes in which the tradition of long years of subjection has enveloped them. They gaze blindly at the carnage or hasten to staunch the blood that flows – as ministering angels, to heal the wounds that the heroism of man has dealt to his brother. . . . The blood flows too fast, it is only some drops that are staunched . . . and meanwhile the bodies are piled higher and higher, the graves are dug deeper and deeper.

Charles Kay Ogden: *Militarism versus Feminism*, 1915

Questions

1   Look carefully at the first sentence of this passage. What view of the traditional role of women, and of how this affected their reaction to war, does it suggest?

2   How is this writer's objection to the war different from the objections of other writers in this section?

The writers quoted in this section all oppose the war in different ways, and their views all differ greatly from the opinions expressed in most of the other contemporary sources in this book. Yet almost all of the writers have one thing in common: they share a realisation that women had the power to influence events by the way they reacted to the war.

By 1918 the way in which women had contributed to the war was clearly having an effect on men's attitudes so that, by the later stages of the fighting, those in authority were at last convinced that women should have a voice in the running of the nation.

The vote

In March 1917, a new Representation of the People Act was proposed in the House of Commons by Herbert Asquith – the man who, as Prime Minister, had refused the vote to women in the years before the war. One clause of the bill gave the vote to women over 30 who were householders or were married to householders. Explaining his change in attitude, Asquith said this about women and the war:

> *How could we have carried on the war without them? Short of actually bearing arms in the field, there is hardly a service which has contributed, or is contributing, to the maintenance of our cause in which women have not been at least as active and as efficient as men, and wherever we turn we see them doing, with zeal and success . . . work which three years ago would have been regarded as falling exclusively within the province of men. This is not merely a sentimental argument, though it appeals to our feelings as well as our judgement. But what I confess moves me still more in this matter is the problem of reconstruction when the War is over. The questions which will then necessarily arise in regard to women's labour and women's functions in the new order of things . . . are questions in regard to which I . . . find it impossible . . . to withhold from women the power and the right of making their voices directly heard.*
> The Parliamentary Debates (Official Report), Fifth Series,
> Vol. XCII, 26 March–27 April 1917

Asquith was not alone in his praise. When the bill became law:

> *. . . there were hearty and general cheers. . . . It [marked] Parliament's appreciation of the splendid services of women in the war.*
> Michael MacDonagh: *In London During the Great War*, 1935

Questions

1 What two reasons does Asquith give for extending the vote to women? Which of the two do you think was the more popular with MPs, to judge from what MacDonagh says?

2   You are a member of the WSPU who has taken part in the
    pre-war suffragette demonstrations to win the vote for women,
    because you feel women should be on equal terms with men.
    Think carefully about how you would react to women being
    given the vote for their 'splendid services' in the war, and then
    write a diary entry for 28 March 1917, the day after Asquith's
    speech, making clear whether you are pleased or angry at the
    news.

Although women had been campaigning for the vote for many years,
when it was achieved it came as an anticlimax. Little was said or
written about it, and the newspapers were more interested in the
latest war news. Perhaps most women were more concerned with
their current and very real hardships, rather than with political issues
which seemed to have little to do with their daily lives. Some,
though, were angry that the vote had been granted as a reward for
war work, rather than in recognition of women's right to the
franchise. One woman reacted like this:

> The vote was 'given' to [women] in 1918 rather as a biscuit is given
> to a performing dog who has just done its tricks particularly well.
> Mrs C.S. Peel: *How We Lived Then, 1914–1918*, 1929

The bill to allow women over 21 to stand for Parliament became law
just before the election in 1918, giving women candidates little
preparation time. Perhaps because of this, only 17 out of the 1 623
candidates were women. Christabel Pankhurst stood as a representa-
tive of the Women's Party, a body formed to continue the aims of
the WSPU. She was not returned to Westminster, and the only
successful woman candidate, Countess Markievicz, refused to take
her seat because, as an Irish Republican, she did not approve of
government from London.

It was not until 1919 that the first woman entered the House of
Commons. Lady Astor fought the Plymouth (Sutton) by-election, as
a Conservative, after her husband had had to resign his seat and
move to the House of Lords when he inherited his father's title.
Some opponents claimed that she had only been elected because her
husband had held the seat before her, but the voters would not have
elected a candidate just for this reason. Lady Astor won because of
her energetic campaigning and deep concern for the local people.

Despite the longer time for campaigning in the 1922 election,
there were still very few women candidates, and only two women
were returned to the House. In the election of 1923, the number rose
to eight, but in the Labour victory of the following year this was
halved. However, towards the end of the decade there was an
important advance. In 1928, Stanley Baldwin's Conservative
administration extended the vote to all women over 21. This meant

Above left: *the 1923 election, Devonport; Liberals campaigning against food taxes. The posters seem to be aimed at women voters; but what view of the role of women do they represent?*

Left: *on the outside looking in? A travelling election office, Southwark, 1929*

Above right: *a threat to the nation? Women of 21 using their freshly won power to vote; Stepney, London, 1929*

Right: *the threshold of power. Margaret Bondfield, Minister of Labour, leaving 10 Downing St. in 1929*

that 3½ million women between the ages of 21 and 30, and another 1.8 million over 30 who were not householders, could vote. It also meant that female voters now outnumbered male voters by 2¼ million.

The popular press was alarmed. The Conservative *Daily Mail* warned about giving the vote to 'impulsive and politically ignorant girls', who might 'dominate the State' and cause 'a national calamity', and there was much correspondence about what was called the 'Flapper Vote' (see page 42). In the 1929 election, 14 women were elected, but what was even more important was that Margaret Bondfield became Minister of Labour. In a Labour Government, this was more than a token appointment; it was an expression of confidence not only in one person, but in the ability of women to occupy high ministerial office. With Labour – traditionally in favour of women in the House – now in power, and a woman in the Cabinet, it seemed that real advances were to be made.

Questions

1   Why do you think so few women stood in the election of 1918? Was it because there was not enough preparation time, or could it have been that women were angry at the way they had been given the vote – or was there some other reason? Discuss your ideas in small groups.

2   What attitude towards women is suggested by the term 'Flapper Vote'? Does this suggest that men's attitudes towards women in politics had changed since the war?

What happened after 1929 did not fulfil the expectations of women in Parliament. The financial crisis of 1931 led to the formation of a National Government – a coalition whose main concern was to pull the country out of depression. The desire for economic recovery squeezed out what little concern there had ever been for greater representation of women in the House and, although there were 15 women MPs in 1931, the number dropped to nine in 1935. Since then, it has never gone above 29 and, though there have been distinguished individual figures such as Ellen Wilkinson, Barbara Castle and Shirley Williams, only since 1974 have there been significantly more than 100 women candidates. The presence of Margaret Thatcher as party leader and Prime Minister has been a triumph for women's representation, but it has done nothing to increase the number of women in the House; in 1986 there were 25 women MPs, compared with 26 to 29 under male leaders in the sixties. The 300 Group, a non-party body campaigning for at least 300 women MPs, feels that an increase in the number of women at Westminster would improve the way things are done in the House of Commons.

Why are there so few women in Parliament? Some feel that the whole educational and social system does not prepare them for the cut and thrust of political debate, since the ideal woman is still presented as gentle, quiet and unassertive. Others suggest that women themselves do not vote for women candidates; or that party selection committees are still male-dominated and rarely choose women to stand for Parliament. Alternatively, perhaps it is the fact that most women feel responsible for the running of the home and family, and thus effectively have to do two jobs:

... even before they go to work they may have to arrange breakfast, do household chores, get children ready and off to school and a husband out to work. Before she starts on a job outside, a woman has generally done a job inside the house. And after work, or in the lunch hour, she is shopping and planning meals ready for the evening. More than any single factor – like child care itself, or housework – it is the general organisation of the life of a family that takes up a major part of most women's energy.... It is clearly necessary for an MP to be able to give his or her wholehearted attention to the job. It was in this context that one of the early women MPs remarked that a wife is the most valuable asset in politics. And a wife is just what a woman doesn't have.

Elisabeth Vallance: *Women in the House; A Study of Women Members of Parliament*, 1979

Women in Parliament			
	Number of women candidates	Number of women elected	Government
1918	17	1	Coalition
1922	33	2	Conservative
1923	34	8	Conservative
1924	41	4	Labour
1929	69	14	Labour
1931	62	15	National
1935	67	9	National
1945	87	24	Labour
1950	126	21	Labour
1951	77	17	Conservative
1955	92	24	Conservative
1959	81	25	Conservative
1964	90	29	Labour
1966	81	26	Labour
1970	99	26	Conservative
1974 (Feb.)	143	23	Labour
1974 (Oct.)	161	27	Labour
1979	206	19	Conservative
1983	276	23	Conservative

Questions

1 Can you find any direct relationship between the number of women standing for Parliament and the number actually elected?

2 Is there any relationship between the party winning the election and the number of women MPs?

3 What do you think the MP meant when she said that 'a wife is the most valuable asset in politics'? What idea of the role of a wife is suggested by this statement?

4 Why do you think so few women have become MPs? Is it for any of the reasons suggested here, or for other reasons, perhaps even a feeling that politics is not really important? Discuss your ideas in small groups.

A lasting achievement?

How should we sum up the achievement of women in World War I? Was it really the turning point that it was thought to be at the time, with women gaining access to many new jobs and professions, and changing for ever the role that they played in the family and in society? Or was it simply a temporary change, with the advances lost after the men returned from the war, when rebuilding lives and relationships shattered by separation and loss seemed more important than struggling on towards equality?

Today, a new generation is continuing the struggle, and the tide is perhaps beginning to turn towards real equality of opportunity. Many feminists feel that not enough was made of the real advances achieved in World War I, and it is fitting that a leading campaigner of this age should sum up the efforts of earlier times:

> ... *it seemed clear that emancipation had failed; the number of women in Parliament had settled at a low level; the number of professional women had stabilized as a tiny minority; the pattern of female employment had emerged as underpaid, menial and supportive. The cage door had been opened and the canary had refused to fly out. The conclusion was that the cage door ought never to have been opened because canaries are made for captivity; the suggestion of an alternative had only confused and saddened them.*
>
> Germaine Greer: *The Female Eunuch*, 1970

Waving flags or dancing in the dark? Women celebrating the end of the war. What different moods do the two photographs suggest? Do they suggest different attitudes to the future? Which do you find the more accurate forecast of the role of women in years to come, and why?

Question

Think about what women achieved during World War I, and the various roles they fulfil today. Compare your views with those expressed in this passage, and discuss your ideas in groups.

INDEX

Numerals in **bold** denote illustrations

Agriculture, women in, 31–3, **32**
Anderson, Louisa Garrett, 23
Asquith, Herbert Henry, 10, 15, 50
Astor, Lady, 51

Baldwin, Stanley, 51
Board of Trade – Conference of Women's Organisations, 12
Bondfield, Margaret, 35, 53, **53**
British Red Cross, 9, 21
Business, women in, 29–30, **30**

Castle, Barbara, 53
Churchill, Winston, 5
Conscientious objectors, 47

Dawson, Margaret, 28
Doctors, women as, 8, 23–4, **24**, 42
Domestic service, women in, **12**, 43

Factory Act, 1874, 14
Factory Inspectors, women, 16
Family life, deterioration of, 40
Fashion, changes in, **42–3**
First Aid Nursing Yeomanry (FANY), 21
'Flapper Vote', 1928, 53
Food, shortages and rationing of, 37, **37**, 38–40, **39**, **40**
Freedom, social, of women during and after war, 41–2

Inglis, Dr Elsie, 10, 23

Keogh, Alfred, 23

Lawrence, Susan, 35
Lloyd George, David, 5, 15, 47

Markievicz, Countess, 51

Marshall, Catherine, 48
Mason, Winnie, **48**
Members of Parliament, women, 51, 53–4
Munitions Tribunals, 47
Munitions, women in, 13, **13**, **16**, 17–20, **18**, **19**, 35, 45, **45**

National Union of Women's Suffrage Societies (NUWSS), 8
No-Conscription Fellowship, 48
Nurses, women as, 9, 21–3, **21**, **22**

Opposition to war, 47–50, **47**, **48**, 49

Pankhurst, Christabel, 5, 6
Pankhurst, Emmeline, 7
Pankhurst, Sylvia, 7, 47
Politics, women and, 50–55, **52**, **53**
Professions, women in, 42
Punch, **12**, **16**

Queen Mary's Army Auxiliary Corps (QMAAC), 27

Recruiting, women and, **8**, **9**
Registration of women, voluntary, 11–12, **12**
Representation of the People Act, 1917, 50
Right-to-Serve Procession, Women's, **5**, 5–6, 7, 15

St John's Ambulance Brigade, 21
Salvage, women unloading, **34**
Secretaries, women as, 8, 29–30, **44**
Sex Disqualification (Removal) Act, 1919, 42
Suffragettes, 7–8, 11
Suffragists, 8

Textiles, women working with, 10
Thatcher, Margaret, 53
300 Group, The, 53
Trade Unions, 11, 14, 15, 43
Transport, women in, 31, **31**
Treasury Agreement, 14

University, women at, 8, 42

Voluntary Aid Detachments (VADs), 21, 22–3, 24, 25

Wages, women's, 38
War Office, 10, 35–6
Wheeldon, Alice, **48**
Wheeldon, Hettie, **48**
Wilkinson, Ellen, 53
Williams, Shirley, 53
Women Police Volunteers, 28
Women's Army Auxiliary Corps (WAAC), 25–7, **26**, **27**
Women's employment
  before World War I, 8, 10
  and official resistance, 6–11
  early in World War I, 11–16
  in World War I, 17–36
  in 1920s, 42–3
  in 1930s, 44
  in World War II, 45
  since 1945, 46
Women's Hospital Corps, 23
Women's Land Army, 32–3
Women's Party, 51
Women's Police Service, 27–9, **28**
Women's Royal Air Force (WRAF), 26
Women's Royal Naval Service (Wrens), 26
Women's Social and Political Union (WSPU), 5, 7, 8, 51
World War II, women and, 45, **45**